mother

baby

brother

sister

me

This is my family.

1

window

tree　　　door

This　is　my　house

swing

slide

① ② sand box

and back yard. 3

lamp

clown

crib

beads

This is my room

4

brush

comb

mirror

rocking chair

② ① ③

play pen

① ②

pull toy

① ②

5

owl

monkey

giraffe

lion

and   my   own

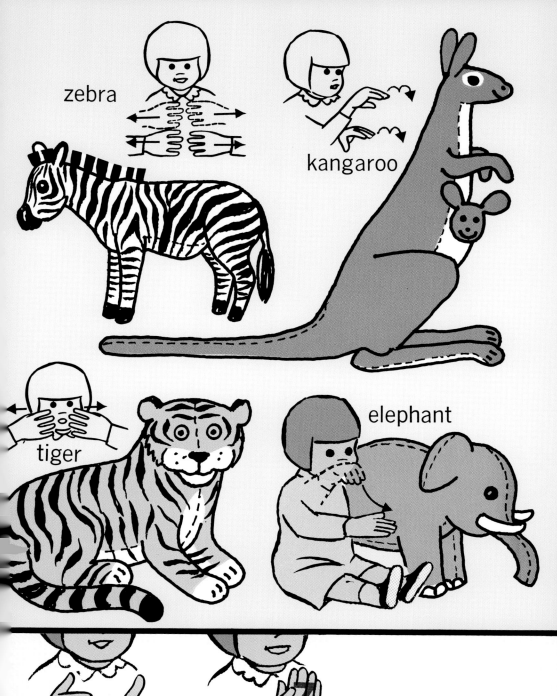

zebra

kangaroo

tiger

elephant

little

zoo.

spoon

bib

cup

egg

cereal

Here I am eating

8

butter

apple ① ② ③ juice

milk

soda

refrigerator

stove

in mommy's kitchen. 9

milk bottle

① ②

orange

banana

sandwich

cookie

These are my

hamburger

french fries

ice cream

lollipop

soup

favorite foods.

② ①

book

T.V.

sofa

This   is   our

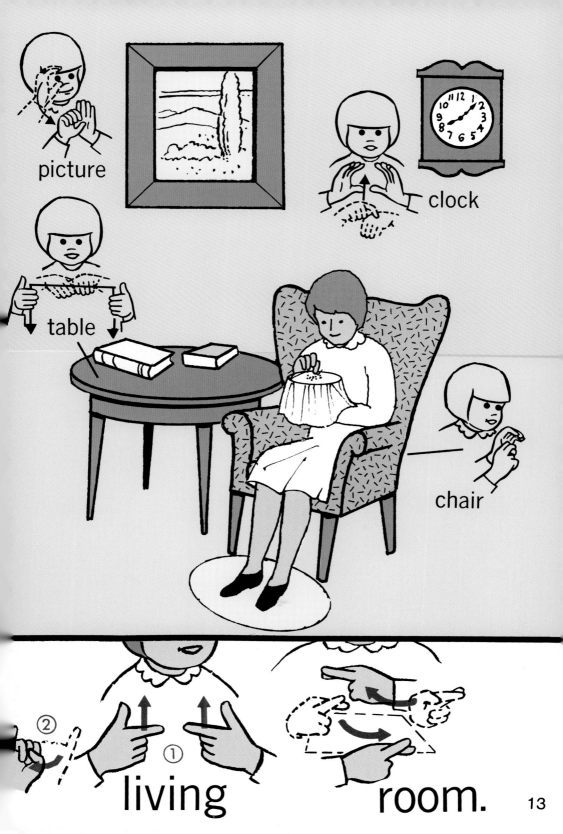

picture

clock

table

chair

② ① living room.

13

sun

bee

flower

bug

worm

Here   I

14

bird

fence

turtle

grasshopper

am outside.

towel

toilet

water

soap

② Baths ① are fun.